To SHARON

BUON Appetito!

Cicciotti's
KITCHEN

Cicciotti's KITCHEN

Italian Family Favorites —
Quick, Easy and Delicious

Gaetano Cicciotti

Photography by Michael D. Pawlenty

 Chefs Press

Published by Chefs Press, San Diego, California
www.chefspress.com

Design by Amy Stirnkorb

ISBN-13: 978-0-9816222-0-0
ISBN-10: 0-9816222-0-8

First Edition
Printed in China

d e d i c a t i o n

Dedicato ai miei fantastici figli.
— Gaetano

contents

foreword

About Cicciotti's Trattoria

I have known Gaetano Cicciotti *(pronounced CHEE-chotti)* for almost 10 years, and am a regular at his restaurant, Cicciotti's Trattoria. You should become one too. I have eaten probably every dish Gaetano has ever created and served. He has even included a few of my favorites in his first cookbook, *Cicciotti's Kitchen* — Carpaccio di Manzo (page 33), Gorgonzola Gnocchi with Toasted Walnuts (page 62), and Lasagne alla Napoletana (page 87). Give these recipes a try in your own kitchen or come enjoy the home-style cooking at Cicciotti's Trattoria. Gaetano has created an oasis, a culinary haven, in San Diego. He takes great care in creating memorable evenings for his guests. It's more than just visiting a great Italian Ristorante; it's a total experience for all your senses.

From the moment you see his trademark tiki torches and panoramic view of the Pacific Ocean, you get a sense this is not going to be dinner as usual. The customary greeting of a handshake pulled into an embrace; the kisses for the ladies on the cheek — all are completely genuine receptions to Cicciotti's. He welcomes customers in a way that you know he values his friendships with patrons. Most evenings, you will find Gaetano circulating from table to table making sure his diners are happy and satisfied. The extensive wine list, the fresh cooked-to-order dishes, and live music blend together with Gaetano's personal touch and commitment to the art of dining well.

Please enjoy cooking the recipes in this cookbook as much as I've enjoyed eating them at Cicciotti's. Salute!

—Kendell Lang

introduction

Fresh & Simple Cooking

I first tasted the joys of Southern Italian cooking as a child growing up in Naples, Italy. Surrounded by simple, fresh ingredients, I loved the time I spent in the kitchen with my mother and grandmother. From them I learned to cherish old world traditions — nostalgic recipes where aromas and tastes transport you back to simpler times. I fondly remember having Baccalà, one of my grandmother's specialties. It is a salted cod dish; and even though it is not a Mediterranean fish, it has always been a favorite of Italians. Another favorite of mine growing up was my mother's Spaghetti alla Carbonara — a classical recipe that's so full of flavor and easy to make. Look for it on page 50.

Ever since I realized my boyhood dream and opened Cicciotti's Trattoria in 2002, easy-to-make, good-tasting food has been especially important to me. I love the smells and sounds of the kitchen, and enjoy experimenting with fresh vegetables from the local farmer's market, leftovers in my refrigerator or the dried pastas in my pantry. I learned an interesting fact at the restaurant early on: back home, Italians enjoy their pastas dry, but in America, more sauce is better.

One new dish I created for Valentine's Day at the restaurant was a luscious lobster and seafood fettuccine dish with fresh live Maine lobster. (See page 95.)

My uncle, Pino, and my mother, Maria, at home in the kitchen.

On another occasion at home, I created a new recipe for dinner for my wife, Monica, and my three children. They loved it so much that I had to include in this cookbook at the last minute. You'll find Torta di Rapini al Forno on page 92.

This is what my cookbook, *Cicciotti's Kitchen*, is all about: sharing some delicious dishes — Italian classics, restaurant favorites and new creations — and showing you how easy they are to make. It's using the fresh, simple staples that I grew up with: fish, cheese, pasta, olive oil, tomato, onion and basil. You'll find all of these ingredients in the recipes throughout this book.

Fill your kitchen with the aromas and tastes that I fondly remember and still create today. Give these recipes a try, and see how you too can create your own new traditions.

Buon Appetito!

"*As a boy, I sat with my mother in the kitchen and watched her cook.*"

SALSE
{SAUCES}

MARINARA SAUCE

m a k e s 2 q u a r t s

- **4 cups finely chopped yellow onions**
- **5 peeled and minced garlic cloves**
- **¼ cup good-quality olive oil**
- **Splash of white wine**
- **Mixed fresh herbs**
  (thyme, oregano, Italian parsley)
- **3 dried bay leaves**
- **3 (28-ounce) cans whole peeled plum**
  tomatoes (with basil if available)
- **Fresh whole basil leaves**
- **4 tablespoons butter, chilled**
- **Salt and freshly ground pepper to taste**

CHEF'S TIP

Photo illustrates covering a pot three quarters. A wooden spoon keeps the lid slightly open and food moist, while allowing some steam to escape.

In a large stockpot over medium heat, sauté the onion and garlic in olive oil until golden brown. Add a splash of white wine. In a piece of cheesecloth or a bouquet garni bag, tie up the fresh herbs and bay leaves; add it to the stockpot along with tomatoes and a few fresh basil leaves. Cover with lid three quarters *(see tip above)*, reduce heat to medium low, and cook for 35 to 45 minutes until sauce has reduced and thickened. Stir occasionally. Season with salt and freshly ground pepper to taste.

Turn off the heat. Remove the bouquet garni, and let cool for about 10 minutes. Stir in butter to finish. Purée sauce in a blender until completely smooth.

Good for 5 to 6 days in the refrigerator.

Good on: All pastas, manicotti

BOLOGNESE SAUCE

makes 2 quarts

4 cups finely chopped yellow onions
¼ cup good-quality olive oil
1 cup butter
½ cup finely chopped celery
½ cup finely chopped carrots
1 pound ground pork
1 pound ground beef
1 cup white wine
2 (15-ounce) cans tomato sauce
Salt and freshly ground pepper to taste

In a large frying pan or stockpot over medium heat, sauté the onion in olive oil and butter until golden brown. Stir in celery and carrots, continue cooking until soft. Then add pork, beef and white wine, and cook for 10 minutes. Add the tomato sauce, cover three quarters, and cook for another 40 to 50 minutes, stirring occasionally.

Turn off the heat. Once the sauce has cooled, skim off the excess fat. Season with salt and freshly ground pepper to taste.

Good for 5 to 6 days in the refrigerator.

Good on: Penne, rigatoni, lasagne, ravioli, cannelloni

PORCINI SAUCE

makes 4 cups

1 cup dried porcini mushrooms
1 finely chopped shallot
2 tablespoons good-quality olive oil
¼ cup brandy
4 cups heavy cream
Salt and freshly ground pepper to taste
Freshly ground nutmeg to taste

Rehydrate mushrooms in warm water for 20 minutes. Drain, and save 1 teaspoon of the mushroom liquid. In a large sauté or frying pan over medium heat, sauté shallots in olive oil, until golden brown. Stir in mushrooms and reserved liquid. Add brandy and flame. Once alcohol has burned off and flame has subsided, stir in heavy cream. Season with salt, freshly ground pepper and nutmeg to taste.

Good for 5 to 6 days covered in the refrigerator.

Good on: Filet of beef, ribeye, lamb chops

BESCIAMELLA SAUCE
{BÉCHAMEL SAUCE}

makes 2 quarts

2 quarts whole milk
2 cups butter
1 cup flour
½ teaspoon freshly ground nutmeg
Salt and freshly ground pepper to taste

In a large stockpot, warm the milk over low to medium heat.

Meanwhile, in a second large stockpot, melt the butter over medium heat.
Whisk in the flour until the mixture becomes paste-like and the raw flour taste
has been cooked out. Slowly add the warm milk, whisking constantly, until it becomes
creamy, about 15 minutes. For a thinner sauce, whisk in more milk to desired
consistency. Season with nutmeg, salt and freshly ground pepper to taste.

Good for 5 to 6 days in the refrigerator.

Good on: Lasagne, cannelloni

ANTIPASTI
{APPETIZERS}

"You either love cooking or you don't. My son is only 4 years old and he loves to cook."

ASPARAGI ALLA ZINGARA
{ASPARAGUS BUNDLES WITH PROSCIUTTO}

serves 4

---

1 sourdough baguette
2 cups homemade Marinara Sauce *(see page 16)*
1 pound fresh asparagus
¼ pound sliced Prosciutto di Parma
8 ounces fresh mozzarella cheese, sliced
Garnish: Freshly grated Parmigiano-Reggiano cheese
Garnish: Fresh basil

Preheat oven to 400 degrees. Slice the baguette, and toast for about 3 to 4 minutes, until crisp. Set aside. Keep oven on.

Meanwhile, heat marinara sauce.

Steam asparagus until al dente, about 2 to 3 minutes. Divide asparagus into 4 bundles, and wrap each bundle in 1 or 2 slices of prosciutto. Place bundles on a baking sheet or shallow roasting pan. Top with sliced mozzarella. Bake until cheese melts, about 3 to 5 minutes.

To serve: Spoon a pool of marinara sauce on a plate. Lay 1 bundle of asparagus on top. Drizzle with more marinara. Serve with toasted baguette slices. Garnish with grated cheese and fresh basil.

BRUSCHETTA ASSORTITA

serves 4

| 1 sourdough baguette
| 2 tablespoons crumbled Gorgonzola cheese
| 4 tablespoons heavy cream
| ¼ pound sliced smoked salmon (Scottish quality)
| ½ cup finely chopped black or Kalamata olives
| 1 cup finely chopped Roma tomatoes
| 3 peeled and minced garlic cloves
| 1 finely chopped shallot
| 1 to 2 tablespoons good-quality extra virgin olive oil
| Salt and freshly ground pepper to taste
| Garnish: Fresh basil

Preheat oven to 400 degrees. Slice the sourdough baguette, and toast for about 3 to 4 minutes, until crisp. Set aside.

Salmon Bruschetta: In a sauce pan over medium heat, stir together the Gorgonzola cheese and heavy cream until the cheese is melted. Spread mixture on baguette slices. Top with salmon.

Kalamata Bruschetta: Chop olives in a food processor. Spread on baguette slices.

Fresh Tomato Bruschetta: Chop tomatoes, garlic and shallot. Stir in olive oil. Season with salt and freshly ground pepper.

Garnish with basil. *(See page 30 for how to make a tomato rosette.)*

OSTRICHE ROCKEFELLER
{OYSTERS ROCKEFELLER}

serves 4

½ cup finely chopped yellow onion
¼ pound pancetta, diced
2 tablespoons good-quality extra virgin olive oil
12 ounces fresh baby spinach
1 cup Besciamella Sauce *(see page 19)*
1 dozen fresh or frozen (thawed) on the half shell oysters
4 tablespoons freshly grated Parmigiano-Reggiano cheese
Garnish: Finely chopped Italian parsley

In a large sauté or frying pan over medium heat, sauté onion and pancetta in olive oil, until crisp. Add spinach. Cover and cook until spinach is wilted. Stir in besciamella sauce.

Preheat oven to 400 degrees. Place oysters on a baking sheet. Top each with spinach mixture and 1 teaspoon of cheese. Bake for 7 to 10 minutes, until cheese is melted and bubbly.

Serve 3 hot oysters per person. Garnish with parsley.

GAMBERI MARGHERITA CON POLENTA
{SHRIMP IN CREAM SAUCE WITH POLENTA}

serves 4

8 cleaned, peeled, tail-on jumbo shrimp
Flour for coating
2 tablespoons good-quality olive oil
½ cup finely chopped yellow onion
Optional for richer sauce: ½ teaspoon lobster or shrimp base or bouillon *(see resources page 96)*
Splash of good brandy
1 cup heavy cream
Salt and freshly ground pepper to taste
Garnish: Fresh basil

Coat shrimp lightly with flour. Set aside. In a large frying pan over medium heat, sauté onion in olive oil until golden brown. If using, add lobster base, then sauté shrimp for about 2 minutes per side, until they turn red. Add splash of brandy and flame it. Once alcohol has burned off and flame has subsided, stir in heavy cream. Cook for 2 more minutes. Do not overcook. Season with salt and freshly ground pepper to taste.

To make polenta: Follow cooking directions on package of instant polenta, plus add 1 cup whole milk to cooking water as you whisk in polenta. Once polenta begins to thicken, stir in 4 tablespoons Gorgonzola, 3 tablespoons butter, ½ cup heavy cream and ¼ cup whole milk. Let cool.

To serve: Pack polenta in buttered espresso cup or other mold. Turn cup upside down on plate to release polenta. Serve 2 shrimp per person with sauce. Top with fresh basil.

INSALATA CAPRESE

serves 4

2-3 round salad tomatoes, sliced
12 fresh basil leaves
1 pound fresh buffalo mozzarella cheese, sliced
Good-quality extra virgin olive oil
Salt and freshly ground pepper to taste
Dried oregano, to taste

To serve: Place 3 slices of tomato on a plate. Place 1 basil leaf on each tomato slice. Then top with 3 slices of mozzarella.

Drizzle with extra virgin olive oil. Season with salt, freshly ground pepper and dried oregano to taste. Top with tomato rosette.

CHEF'S TIP

To make a tomato rosette: Peel 1 small round salad tomato with a sharp paring knife, rotating clockwise, as you would peel an apple. Be careful not to break the tomato peel while you are rotating and peeling. Then take the peel and arrange it in a circle to create the rose.

CARPACCIO DI MANZO
{BEEF CARPACCIO}

serves 4

16 ounces thinly sliced fresh filet mignon (have butcher slice meat)
3½ ounces baby arugula
Shaved Parmigiano-Reggiano cheese
¼ cup capers, drained
3 tablespoons good-quality extra virgin olive oil
Salt and freshly ground pepper to taste
1 fresh lemon, squeezed for juice
Garnish: Lemon wedges

To serve: Place sliced meat, pile of arugula, and shaved Parmigiano-Reggiano on a plate. Sprinkle a few capers on top. Drizzle with olive oil. Season with salt, freshly ground pepper and a squeeze of lemon. Serve with fresh lemon wedges on the side.

CHEF'S TIP

Extra-virgin olive oil comes from virgin oil production only.
It has a superior taste, and is best for garnishing and finishing dishes.

Pure olive oil is a blend of refined and virgin production oil.
It doesn't have as strong a flavor as virgin olive oils, and is best for cooking.

ZUPPE

{SOUP}

*"Fresh,
quality
ingredients
are key
to Italian
cooking."*

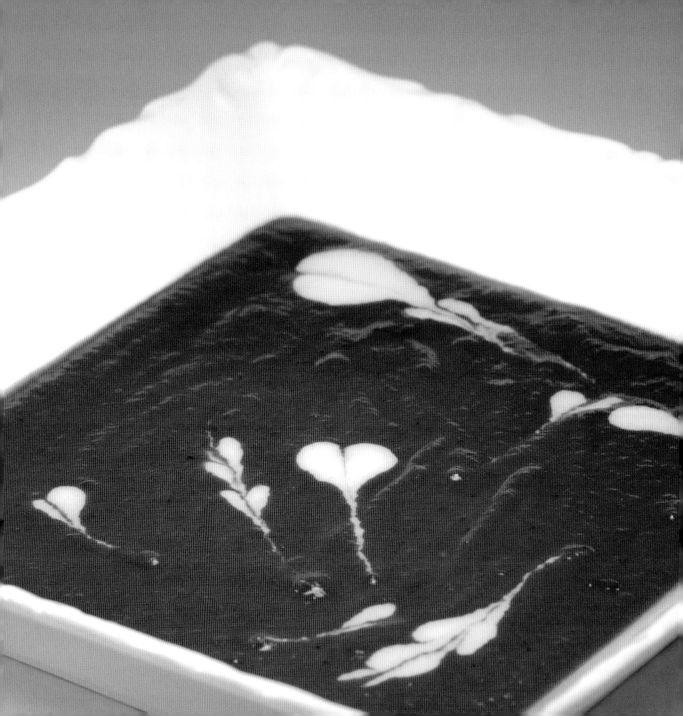

CREMA DI POMODORI
{TOMATO CREAM SOUP}

serves 4

> **4 cups Marinara Sauce** *(see page 16)*
> **4 tablespoons heavy cream**
> **3 tablespoons finely chopped fresh basil**
> **Salt and freshly ground pepper to taste**
> Garnish: Fresh basil
> Garnish: Homemade croutons

In a large sauté or frying pan over medium heat, combine the marinara sauce, cream and basil; heat for 4 to 5 minutes, and bring to a boil. Season with salt and freshly ground pepper to taste. Garnish with fresh basil and homemade croutons.

To create decorative heart design on soup: Drizzle 1 to 2 tablespoons of Besciamella Sauce *(see page 19)* in pattern on top of soup. Take a toothpick and drag it through the center of the besciamella to create the hearts.

CHEF'S TIP

To make homemade croutons: Cut a loaf of bread or baguette into small cubes; remove crusts. In a large bowl, toss cubes with 2 tablespoons melted butter, and seasoning of your choice (dried herbs, garlic, salt and freshly ground pepper). Bake for about 10 minutes at 400 degrees until crisp and golden.

STRACCIATELLA
{SPINACH & EGG SOUP}

serves 4

24 ounces fresh baby spinach
2 tablespoons good-quality olive oil
4 cups chicken broth
4 whole eggs (use pasteurized)
Salt and freshly ground pepper to taste
Garnish: Freshly grated Parmigiano-Reggiano cheese
Garnish: Homemade croutons *(see page 37)*

In a large sauté or frying pan over medium heat, sauté spinach in olive oil for 1 to 2 minutes. Cover three quarters and steam for about 5 minutes. Add broth. Bring to a boil. Stir in eggs and gently scramble until cooked, about 2 to 3 minutes. Season with salt and freshly ground pepper to taste.

Garnish with grated Parmigiano-Reggiano cheese and homemade croutons.

ZUPPETTA DI COZZE, VONGOLE E CAPESANTE
{MUSSEL, CLAM & SCALLOP SOUP}

serves 4

½ cup finely chopped yellow onion
2 tablespoons good-quality olive oil
2 cups finely chopped Roma tomatoes
½ pound fresh or frozen (thawed) black or green mussels, cleaned
1 pound fresh or frozen (thawed) Manila clams, cleaned
½ pound fresh or frozen (thawed) large bay scallops, cleaned
1 cup white wine
Salt and freshly ground pepper to taste
Garnish: Chopped Italian parsley

In a large sauté or frying pan over medium heat, sauté onion in olive oil until soft. Stir in tomatoes and cook for 2 minutes. Add seafood. Cover three quarters and cook for 5 minutes. Add wine, continue to cook covered for about 5 more minutes, until seafood is fully cooked. Discard any clams or mussels that do not open. Season with salt and freshly ground pepper to taste.

Garnish with parsley. Serve with toasted baguette slices on the side.

ZUPPA DI CARCIOFI
{ARTICHOKE SOUP}

serves 4

½ cup finely chopped yellow onion
2 tablespoons good-quality olive oil
1 cup chopped Roma tomatoes
14 ounces whole artichoke hearts, quartered
4 cups chicken broth
¼ cup julienned fresh basil
Salt and freshly ground pepper to taste
Garnish: Freshly grated Parmigiano-Reggiano cheese
Garnish: Homemade croutons *(see page 37)*

In a large sauté or frying pan over medium heat, sauté the onion in olive oil until soft. Stir in tomatoes and cook for 5 minutes. Add artichoke hearts, cooking for 2 to 3 more minutes. Add broth and basil. Bring to a boil. Season with salt and freshly ground pepper to taste.

Garnish with grated Parmigiano-Reggiano cheese and homemade croutons.

ZUPPA DI ZUCCHINE
{ZUCCHINI SOUP}

serves 4

½ cup finely chopped yellow onion
2 tablespoons good-quality olive oil
3 large zucchini, cut into small pieces
1 large russet potato, peeled and cut into small pieces
4 cups chicken broth
2 to 3 small dried porcini mushrooms
Salt and freshly ground pepper to taste
¼ teaspoon freshly ground nutmeg
2 tablespoons good brandy
Garnish: Finely chopped Italian parsley
Garnish: Freshly grated Parmigiano-Reggiano cheese
Garnish: Homemade croutons (*see page 37*)

CHEF'S TIP

Replace zucchini with 2 pounds chopped cauliflower; or 2 pounds broccoli florets; or 2 peeled and chopped large eggplants; or 2 pounds trimmed asparagus.

In a large sauté pan or stockpot over medium heat, sauté onion in olive oil until golden brown. Add zucchini and potato, and cook for about 5 minutes. Add broth, cover three quarters, and cook for another 40 minutes.

In a small pan, rehydrate the porcini mushrooms in about ½ cup of warm water. Drain, then add the mushrooms to the stockpot. Season with salt and freshly ground pepper to taste. Remove from heat, and cool. Then purée in blender in batches until completely smooth. Place puréed soup into a second stockpot, and reheat for 5 to 10 minutes. Stir in nutmeg and brandy. Season again with salt and freshly ground pepper to taste. Garnish with parsley, grated Parmigiano-Reggiano cheese and homemade croutons.

PASTE
{PASTA}

"A tavola non si invecchia mai...."

{Time stops when you sit and eat}.

PENNE ALL'AMATRICIANA
{PENNE WITH PANCETTA, ONION & TOMATOES}

serves 4

½ pound pancetta, diced
½ cup finely chopped yellow onion
2 tablespoons good-quality olive oil
Splash of white wine
2 (15-ounce) cans crushed tomatoes
1 teaspoon tomato paste
1 pound penne rigate
½ cup freshly grated Pecorino Romano cheese
Freshly ground black pepper to taste
Garnish: Fresh basil
Garnish: Freshly grated Pecorino Romano cheese

In a large sauté or frying pan over medium heat, cook the pancetta and onion in olive oil until pancetta is crisp and onions are golden brown. Add a splash of white wine and tomatoes. Reduce heat to medium and cook for 20 to 30 minutes. In a small cup, dissolve tomato paste in a touch of water. Stir into sauce.

Meanwhile, cook the pasta in a large pot of boiling salted water until al dente. Drain the pasta lightly, leaving it slightly wet. Add the cooked pasta to the sauce in the sauté pan. Stir in cheese, and toss until the cheese melts and the sauce coats the pasta. Season with freshly ground black pepper to taste.

Garnish with fresh basil and more grated Pecorino Romano cheese.

SPAGHETTI ALLA CARBONARA

serves 4

| ½ pound pancetta, diced
| 2 tablespoons good-quality olive oil
| 4 egg yolks (use pasteurized eggs)
| 1 cup heavy cream
| ½ cup freshly grated Pecorino Romano cheese
| Freshly ground pepper
| 1 pound dried Italian spaghetti
| Garnish: Fresh basil
| Garnish: Freshly grated Pecorino Romano cheese

In a large sauté or frying pan over medium heat, cook the pancetta in olive oil until pancetta is crisp. Remove pan from heat.

In a bowl, lightly beat egg yolks. Stir in cream, Pecorino Romano cheese and a touch of pepper. Set aside.

Meanwhile, cook the pasta in a large pot of boiling salted water until al dente. Drain the pasta lightly, leaving it slightly wet.

Combine the pasta and pancetta over high heat in the sauté pan. Turn off heat. Stir in the egg and cheese mixture. Toss until the sauce coats the pasta.

Garnish with fresh basil and more grated Pecorino Romano cheese.

FETTUCCINE ALFREDO CON POLLO
{FETTUCCINE WITH CREAM SAUCE & CHICKEN}

serves 4

2 chicken breasts, diced
2 tablespoons good-quality olive oil
Splash of brandy
2 cups Besciamella Sauce *(see page 19)*
1 cup heavy cream
1 pound dried egg noodle fettuccine
Salt and freshly ground pepper to taste
Garnish: Fresh basil
Garnish: Freshly grated Parmigiano-Reggiano cheese

CHEF'S TIP

Replace chicken with 16 medium tiger shrimp, and sauté in olive oil for 2 to 5 minutes.

In a large sauté or frying pan over medium heat, sauté chicken in olive oil with a splash of brandy until almost cooked through, about 5 to 10 minutes. Stir in besciamella sauce and heavy cream, and cook for another 5 minutes.

Meanwhile, cook the pasta in a large pot of boiling salted water until al dente. Drain the pasta lightly, leaving it slightly wet. Add the cooked pasta to the sauce in the sauté pan, and toss until the sauce coats the pasta. Season with salt and freshly ground pepper to taste.

Garnish with fresh basil and grated Parmigiano-Reggiano cheese.

TRENETTE AL PESTO CON PINOLI
{FETTUCCINE WITH PESTO & PINE NUTS}

serves 4

2 cups pesto sauce
½ cup heavy cream
1 pound egg noodle fettuccine
½ cup freshly grated Parmigiano-Reggiano cheese
½ cup toasted pine nuts
Salt and freshly ground pepper to taste
Garnish: Fresh basil
Garnish: Freshly grated Parmigiano-Reggiano cheese

In a large sauté or frying pan over medium heat, combine the pesto sauce and cream. Heat until warmed.

Meanwhile, cook the pasta in a large pot of boiling salted water until al dente. Drain the pasta lightly, leaving it slightly wet. Add the cooked pasta to the sauce in the sauté pan. Stir in cheese and pine nuts, and toss until the cheese melts and the sauce coats the pasta. Season with salt and freshly ground pepper to taste. Garnish with fresh basil and more grated Parmigiano-Reggiano cheese.

To make pesto sauce: In blender or food processor combine ½ cup good-quality olive oil, 4 cups packed fresh basil leaves, 1 cup chopped fresh Italian parsley, ½ cup pine nuts, 6 peeled garlic cloves, 1 teaspoon anchovy paste until mixture becomes light green and creamy. Season with salt and freshly ground pepper to taste. Makes about 2 cups.

PENNE ALLA VODKA

serves 4

½ cup finely chopped yellow onion
4 tablespoons butter
1 cup finely chopped Roma tomatoes
½ cup vodka
4 cups Marinara Sauce *(see page 16)*
¼ cup heavy cream
1 pound penne rigate
½ cup freshly grated Parmigiano-Reggiano cheese
½ cup finely chopped fresh basil
Salt and freshly ground pepper to taste
Garnish: Fresh basil
Garnish: Freshly grated Parmigiano-Reggiano cheese

In a large sauté or frying pan over medium heat, sauté onion in butter until soft. Stir in tomatoes and cook for about 5 minutes. Add vodka and flame. Once alcohol has burned off and flame has subsided, stir in marinara sauce and cream. Reduce heat, simmer until warmed together.

Meanwhile, cook the pasta in a large pot of boiling salted water until al dente. Drain the pasta lightly, leaving it slightly wet. Add the cooked pasta to the sauce in the sauté pan. Stir in cheese and basil, and toss until the cheese melts and the sauce coats the pasta. Season with salt and freshly ground pepper to taste.

Garnish with fresh basil and more grated Parmigiano-Reggiano cheese.

RIGATONI CON MELANZANE E SALSICCA
{RIGATONI WITH EGGPLANT & SAUSAGE}

serves 4

1 sliced garlic clove
2 tablespoons good-quality olive oil
½ large eggplant, cut into cubes
2 medium-size sweet Italian sausage links, sliced into rounds
½ cup white wine
4 cups Marinara Sauce *(see page 16)*
Salt and freshly ground pepper to taste
1 pound rigatoni
Garnish: Fresh basil
Garnish: Freshly grated Parmigiano-Reggiano cheese

In a large sauté or frying pan over medium heat, sauté garlic in olive oil until golden brown. Add eggplant and sliced sausage; sauté for 3 to 4 minutes. Add wine, cover three quarters and cook for another 10 minutes, until sausage is completely cooked. Stir in marinara sauce, and cook for another 5 minutes until sauce is hot. Season with salt and freshly ground pepper to taste.

Meanwhile, cook the pasta in a large pot of boiling salted water until al dente. Drain the pasta lightly, leaving it slightly wet. Add the cooked pasta to the sauce in the sauté pan, and toss until the sauce coats the pasta.

Garnish with fresh basil and grated Parmigiano-Reggiano cheese.

FARFALLE ALLA BOSCAIOLA
{BOWTIE PASTA WITH HAM & PEAS}

serves 4

4 tablespoons butter
½ pound diced smoked ham
8 ounces sliced fresh mushrooms
Splash of brandy
8 ounces sweet green peas, drained
2 cups heavy cream
1 pound farfalle (bowtie pasta)
½ cup freshly grated Parmigiano-Reggiano cheese
Salt and freshly ground pepper to taste
Garnish: Fresh basil
Garnish: Freshly grated Parmigiano-Reggiano cheese

In a large sauté or frying pan over medium heat, melt butter and sauté ham until golden brown, about 2 to 3 minutes. Add mushrooms. Add brandy and flame. Once alcohol has burned off and flame has subsided, stir in peas. Cover three quarters and cook for 5 minutes. Stir in heavy cream, and cook for another 10 minutes.

Meanwhile, cook the pasta in a large pot of boiling salted water until al dente. Drain the pasta completely. Add the cooked pasta and cheese to the sauce, and toss until the cheese melts and the sauce coats the pasta. Season with salt and freshly ground pepper to taste.

Garnish with fresh basil and grated Parmigiano-Reggiano cheese.

GORGONZOLA GNOCCHI WITH TOASTED WALNUTS

serves 4

1½ cups crumbled Gorgonzola cheese
2 cups heavy cream
2 pounds dry potato gnocchi
Freshly ground pepper to taste
Garnish: ½ cup toasted chopped walnuts
Garnish: Fresh julienned basil
Garnish: Freshly grated Parmigiano-Reggiano cheese

In a large sauté or frying pan over medium heat, stir together the Gorgonzola cheese and heavy cream until the cheese is melted and sauce is heated through.

Meanwhile, cook gnocchi in a large pot of boiling salted water. When the gnocchi rise to the surface, they are done. Add the gnocchi to the sauce in the sauté pan, and toss until the sauce coats the pasta. Season with freshly ground pepper to taste. Garnish with walnuts, basil and Parmigiano-Reggiano cheese.

CHEF'S TIP

Try Sorrentina-Style Gnocchi: In a large sauté pan over medium heat, combine 2 cups Marinara Sauce (see page 16), 16 ounces chopped fresh mozzarella cheese, ½ cup freshly grated Parmigiano-Reggiano cheese, and 2 tablespoons julienned basil until cheese melts and sauce is heated through. Stir in cooked gnocchi. Place pan in preheated 400-degree oven for 5 to 10 minutes, until top of gnocchi is crisp.

PENNE ALLA PUTTANESCA
{PENNE WITH GARLIC, OLIVES & CAPERS}

serves 4

> 2 sliced garlic cloves
> 3 tablespoons good-quality olive oil
> 1 cup sliced Kalamata olives
> ¼ cup capers, drained
> 2 to 3 tablespoons julienned fresh basil
> Splash of white wine
> 4 cups Marinara Sauce *(see page 16)*
> 1 pound penne rigate
> Salt and freshly ground pepper to taste
> Garnish: Fresh basil
> Garnish: Freshly grated Parmigiano-Reggiano cheese

In a large sauté or frying pan over medium heat, sauté the garlic in olive oil until golden brown. Add olives, capers, basil, splash of white wine and cook covered three quarters, for 3 to 4 minutes. Add marinara sauce and cook for about another 10 minutes.

Meanwhile, cook the pasta in a large pot of boiling salted water until al dente. Drain the pasta. Add the cooked pasta to the sauce in the sauté pan, and toss until the sauce coats the pasta. Season with salt and freshly ground pepper to taste.

Garnish with fresh basil and grated Parmigiano-Reggiano cheese.

PENNETTE DELLO CHEF
{SUN-DRIED TOMATO & GORGONZOLA PASTA}

serves 4

1 diced chicken breast
Flour for coating
½ cup finely chopped yellow onion
2 tablespoons good-quality olive oil
½ cup julienned sun-dried tomatoes
2 tablespoons julienned fresh basil
½ cup crumbled Gorgonzola cheese
½ cup brandy
2 cups heavy cream
1 pound pennette
Salt and freshly ground pepper to taste
Garnish: Fresh basil
Garnish: Freshly grated Parmigiano-Reggiano cheese

Coat chicken lightly in flour. Set aside. In a large sauté or frying pan over medium heat, sauté onion in olive oil until golden brown. Add chicken and cook for about 5 minutes. Stir in sun-dried tomatoes, basil and Gorgonzola. Add brandy and flame. Once alcohol has burned off and flame has subsided, cook for 5 more minutes, then stir in heavy cream.

Meanwhile, cook the pasta in a large pot of boiling salted water until al dente. Drain the pasta lightly, leaving it slightly wet. Add the cooked pasta to the sauce in the sauté pan, and toss until the sauce coats the pasta. Season with salt and freshly ground pepper to taste. Garnish with fresh basil and grated Parmigiano-Reggiano cheese.

LINGUINE AI FRUTTI DI MARE
{SEAFOOD LINGUINE}
serves 4

2 sliced garlic cloves
3 tablespoons good-quality olive oil
3 pounds of mixed fresh seafood (mussels, clams, shrimp, calamari, salmon & white fish)
2 cups white wine
¼ cup chopped fresh Italian parsley
2 cups **Marinara Sauce** *(see page 16)*
1 pound linguine
Salt and freshly ground pepper to taste
Garnish: Fresh Italian parsley
Garnish: Freshly grated Parmigiano-Reggiano cheese

In a large sauté or frying pan over medium heat, sauté garlic in olive oil for just
1 minute, then add all the seafood at once, and continue cooking for 4 to 5 minutes,
stirring frequently. Stir in white wine, parsley and cook for 10 to 12 minutes, until
the shellfish is open and fish is completely cooked. Discard any that do not open.
Add marinara sauce, cover three quarters and cook for another 3 to 4 minutes.

Meanwhile, cook the pasta in a large pot of boiling salted water until al dente.
Drain the pasta lightly, leaving it slightly wet. Add the cooked pasta to the sauce and
seafood in the sauté pan, and toss until the sauce coats the pasta. Season with salt
and freshly ground pepper to taste.

Garnish with parsley and grated Parmigiano-Reggiano cheese.

"In Italy, every family knows how to cook. We would go out to restaurants only for special occasions."

SPECIALITÀ

{SPECIALTIES}

TORTINO DI MELANZANE
{EGGPLANT CAKE}

serves 4

> 2 large eggplants, sliced into 12 rounds
> 3 eggs, lightly beaten
> Flour for coating
> ⅓ cup good-quality olive oil
> 12 large fresh basil leaves
> 8 ounces shredded mozzarella cheese
> 1 cup **Marinara Sauce** *(see page 16)*
> ½ cup **Besciamella Sauce** *(see page 19)*
> Garnish: Fresh basil

Dip eggplant in lightly beaten eggs, then coat lightly in flour. In a large sauté pan over medium heat, fry eggplant slices in olive oil until golden brown, about 4 to 5 minutes. Remove from pan; cool on paper towels.

Preheat oven to 400 degrees. On a baking sheet, layer 1 slice of eggplant, then 1 basil leaf, and a generous sprinkling of shredded mozzarella; repeat two more times to create the tower. Bake for 3 to 4 minutes, until cheese melts.

Meanwhile, heat marinara and besciamella sauces in two small saucepans.

To serve: Spoon a pool of marinara sauce on a plate. While the eggplant tower is still hot, use a large spatula to carefully transfer it onto the plate. Drizzle besciamella sauce over the top. Garnish with fresh basil.

MANICOTTI AL FORNO
{ROLLED PASTA WITH SPINACH & CHEESE}

serves 4

12 ounces fresh baby spinach, steamed
½ cup freshly grated Parmigiano-Reggiano cheese
6 cups ricotta cheese
Salt and freshly ground pepper to taste
4 sheets fresh (or precooked frozen) lasagne sheets *(see recipe below; resources page 96)*
2 cups Besciamella Sauce *(see page 19)*
2 cups Marinara Sauce *(see page 16)*
Garnish: Fresh basil
Garnish: Freshly grated Parmigiano-Reggiano cheese

Preheat oven to 400 degrees. In a large bowl, combine spinach, Parmigiano-Reggiano and ricotta cheese. Season with salt and freshly ground pepper to taste. Lay out lasagne sheet. Spoon 2 cups of mixture onto sheet, then roll up. Cut in half. Place on baking sheet. Cover with both sauces and bake for about 10 minutes.

Serve 2 manicotti per person. Garnish with basil and Parmigiano-Reggiano cheese.

CHEF'S TIP

To make fresh pasta: In a food processor, combine 3 cups all-purpose flour, 4 lightly beaten large eggs, 1 teaspoon salt and 2 tablespoons water just until mixtures begins to form a ball. If dough is too dry, add drops of water as needed, so that dough is firm and not sticky. Then process dough for 15 more seconds. Let dough rest on floured surface for about 1 hour before rolling dough into sheets. Roll out by hand or follow the instructions on your pasta machine.

POLLO AL MARSALA
{CHICKEN WITH MARSALA SAUCE}

serves 4

> 4 boneless skinless chicken breasts
> Flour for coating
> 2 tablespoons good-quality olive oil
> 8 ounces sliced white button mushrooms
> Optional for richer sauce: ½ teaspoon chicken base or bouillon *(see resources page 96)*
> 1 cup sweet cooking Marsala wine
> Salt and freshly ground pepper to taste
> 4 tablespoons butter, chilled
> Garnish: Fresh Italian parsley

Pound chicken breasts to desired thickness. Coat lightly in flour. In a large sauté pan over medium heat, pan fry chicken in olive oil until golden brown, about 2 to 3 minutes per side. Add sliced mushrooms, and if using, stir in chicken base. Cook for 2 to 3 more minutes until mushrooms are just tender. Add Marsala wine, cover three quarters, and cook until chicken is completely done, about 10 minutes.

Season with salt and freshly ground pepper to taste. Stir in butter to finish sauce, and simmer for another 1 to 2 minutes.

Garnish with fresh parsley.

CANNELLONI AL FORNO
{ROLLED PASTA WITH BEEF & SPINACH}

serves 4

½ cup finely chopped yellow onion
2 tablespoons good-quality olive oil
2 pounds ground beef (also can use mix of pork or chicken)
1 cup white wine
12 ounces fresh baby spinach, steamed
1 cup ricotta cheese
½ cup freshly grated Parmigiano-Reggiano cheese
Salt and freshly ground pepper to taste
2 cups Besciamella Sauce *(see page 19)*
2 cups Bolognese Sauce *(see page 17)*
4 sheets fresh (or precooked frozen) lasagne sheets *(see recipe page 75; resources page 96)*
Garnish: Fresh basil
Garnish: Freshly grated Parmigiano-Reggiano cheese

Preheat oven to 400 degrees. In a large sauté or frying pan over medium heat, sauté onion in olive oil until golden brown. Stir in meat and wine; cook for 20 minutes, until well browned. Let cool.

In a large bowl, combine spinach, meat, ricotta and Parmigiano-Reggiano cheese. Season with salt and freshly ground pepper to taste.

Lay out lasagne sheet. Spoon 2 cups of mixture onto sheet, then roll up. Cut in half. Place cannelloni on baking sheet. Cover with both sauces and bake for 10 minutes. Serve 2 cannelloni per person. Top with extra besciamella and bolognese sauce. Garnish with basil and Parmigiano-Reggiano cheese.

SCAMPI ALLA LIVORNESE
{SHRIMP WITH CAPERS & OLIVES}

serves 4

16 large cleaned, butterflied, tail-on shrimp
Flour for coating
2 tablespoons good-quality olive oil
½ cup sliced Kalamata olives
2 tablespoons capers, drained
½ cup fresh julienned basil
1 cup white wine
4 tablespoons butter, chilled
Salt and freshly ground pepper to taste
Garnish: Fresh basil

Coat shrimp lightly in flour. In a large sauté or frying pan over medium heat, sauté shrimp in olive oil for 2 to 3 minutes. Add olives, capers, basil and white wine. Cook covered for 4 to 5 minutes, until shrimp are completely cooked. Stir in butter to finish sauce. Season with salt and freshly ground pepper to taste.

Serve 4 shrimp per person. Garnish with fresh basil.

PICCATA DI POLLO
{CHICKEN WITH LEMON-BUTTER SAUCE}

serves 4

| 4 boneless skinless chicken breasts
Flour for coating
2 tablespoons good-quality olive oil
4 tablespoons capers, drained
8 tablespoons butter
Salt and freshly ground pepper to taste
½ cup white wine
1 large lemon, squeezed for the juice
Garnish: Fresh Italian parsley
Garnish: Fresh lemon slices

Pound chicken to desired thickness. Coat lightly in flour. In a large sauté or frying pan over medium heat, cook chicken in olive oil for 2 to 3 minutes on each side until golden brown. Add capers, butter, salt and freshly ground pepper to taste. Add wine, cover three quarters and cook for 5 minutes. Add lemon juice and cook for another 3 minutes, until chicken is cooked completely through.

Garnish with fresh Italian parsley and lemon slices.

OSSOBUCO DI AGNELLO
{BRAISED LAMB SHANK}

serves 4

5 or 6 dried porcini mushrooms
4 lamb shanks (about 1 pound each)
Flour for coating
½ cup good-quality olive oil
1 cup finely chopped onion
½ cup finely chopped celery
¼ cup finely chopped carrots

2 cups white wine
1 (32-ounce) can whole peeled tomatoes
Mixed fresh herbs (thyme, oregano, Italian parsley, rosemary)
3 dried bay leaves
4 tablespoons butter
Garnish: Fresh rosemary

In a small pan, rehydrate mushrooms in about ½ cup of warm water. Drain; set aside. Lightly coat lamb shanks in flour. In a large frying pan or stockpot over medium to medium-high heat, cook lamb shanks in olive oil, until golden brown on each side. Add onion, celery, carrots and mushrooms, and sauté until golden brown. In a piece of cheesecloth or a bouquet garni bag, tie up the fresh herbs and bay leaves; add it, wine and tomatoes to the pot. Make sure meat is completely covered with liquid (add more wine or water, if needed). Cover three quarters and turn heat down to medium to medium-low. Cook for 3 to 3½ hours until meat falls apart. Check regularly to make sure meat doesn't burn. Remove bouquet garni, and stir in butter to finish. Serve over risotto. Garnish with fresh sprig of rosemary.

CHEF'S TIP

To make risotto: In a stockpot, warm up 4 cups of chicken broth. In a second stockpot over medium heat, sauté 1 cup finely chopped yellow onions in 2 tablespoons good-quality olive oil, until golden brown. Add ½ pound arborio rice, stir regularly, adding in 1 cup of broth at a time, until the liquid is absorbed, about 15 to 20 minutes. Stir in a couple pinches of saffron until risotto is yellow, and cook for 2 to 3 more minutes.

LASAGNE ALLA NAPOLETANA

serves 4

> **2 pounds small meatballs**
> **4 cups Marinara Sauce** *(see page 16)*
> **4 sheets fresh (or precooked frozen) lasagne sheets** *(see recipe page 75; resources page 96)*
> **2 cups Besciamella Sauce** *(see page 19)*
> **2 cups ricotta cheese**
> **2 cups grated mozzarella cheese**
> **1 cup freshly grated Parmigiano-Reggiano cheese**
> Garnish: Fresh basil
> Garnish: Freshly grated Parmigiano-Reggiano cheese

Preheat oven to 400 degrees. Slice meatballs in half.

In a glass baking dish, begin layering. First, ladle a thin layer of marinara sauce. Next place a lasagne sheet on top. Then thin layers of meatballs; marinara sauce; besciamella sauce; ricotta cheese; and sprinkling of both mozzarella and Parmigiano-Reggiano cheese. Repeat layering until dish is nearly full, ending with the mozzarella and parmesan cheese. Bake, covered with foil, for about 30 minutes. Let cool for a few minutes before cutting.

To serve: Spoon a pool of besciamella sauce on a plate. Then place a square of lasagne, and top with more warmed marinara sauce. Garnish with fresh basil and more grated Parmigiano-Reggiano cheese.

PENNETTE ALLA GENOVESE NAPOLETANA
{PENNETTE WITH BRAISED BEEF & ONIONS}

serves 4

> 2 cups thinly sliced yellow onions
> ¼ pound pancetta, diced
> 4 tablespoons good-quality olive oil
> Flour for coating
> 1½ pounds beef shank beef or shoulder
> 3 cups white wine
> 1 pound pennette
> Salt and freshly ground pepper to taste
> Garnish: Fresh basil
> Garnish: Freshly grated Parmigiano-Reggiano cheese

In a large stockpot over medium heat, sauté onion and pancetta in olive oil until golden brown. Lightly coat the meat in flour, then add to the pot. Brown on all sides. Add the wine, completely covering the meat. If necessary add extra water. Leave at medium heat. Cover three quarters, and cook for about 3 hours. Then remove cover, and continue cooking for 20 to 30 minutes, until sauce has reduced and thickened. Season with salt and freshly ground pepper to taste.

Meanwhile, cook the pasta in a large pot of boiling salted water until al dente. Drain the pasta. Set aside.

To plate: Add a serving of pasta to a plate. Lightly shred the meat, and place on top of the pasta. Add more sauce. Garnish with basil and Parmigiano-Reggiano cheese.

SALMONE ALLE OLIVE GRECHE
{SALMON WITH GREEK OLIVES}

serves 4

- **6 ounces Kalamata olives**
- **6 ounces California olives**
- **1 sliced garlic clove**
- **4 tablespoons good-quality olive oil**
- **24 ounces fresh baby spinach**
- **4 skinless salmon filets (8 to 10 ounces each)**
- **Flour for coating**
- **1 cup white wine**
- **Salt and freshly ground pepper to taste**
- **Garnish: Fresh basil**
- **Garnish: Fresh lemon**
- **Garnish: Freshly grated Parmigiano-Reggiano cheese**

Blend olives in food processor or mixer until finely chopped. Set aside. In a large sauté or frying pan over medium heat, sauté garlic in 2 tablespoons of olive oil for 1 to 2 minutes. Add spinach, reduce heat to low, cover and cook for about 20 minutes until spinach is wilted. Meanwhile, lightly coat salmon in flour. In a large sauté or frying pan over medium heat, sauté salmon in remaining olive oil for 2 to 3 minutes on each side. Add wine, cover three quarters, and cook for about 20 minutes, until desired doneness.

To serve: Place a bed of spinach on a plate, then 1 salmon filet, and about 1 tablespoon of the olive paste. Season with salt and freshly ground pepper to taste. Garnish with fresh basil, lemon and more grated Parmigiano-Reggiano cheese.

TORTA DI RAPINI AL FORNO
{BAKED BROCCOLI RABE & SAUSAGE}

serves 4

2 sliced garlic cloves
4 tablespoons good-quality olive oil
Pinch of red pepper flakes
2 bunches fresh rapini or broccoli rabe
   (cleaned, stems removed)
5 fresh mild Italian sausage links
2 cups white wine
½ cup water
2 frozen pastry/pie dough sheets
½ cup freshly grated Parmigiano-Reggiano cheese
1 egg, lightly beaten

> **CHEF'S TIP**
>
> *Stir in 1 cup chopped smoked mozzarella cheese into rapini and sausage mixture before baking.*

Preheat oven to 400 degrees. In a large sauté or frying pan over medium heat, sauté garlic in 2 tablespoons of olive oil until golden brown. Add red pepper flakes. Reduce heat to medium low, and add rapini. Cover three quarters, and cook for 30 minutes.

Meanwhile, in another large sauté pan over medium heat, brown sausage in remaining olive oil for about 5 minutes. Add white wine and water; cover three quarters, and cook for about 30 minutes. Let sausage cool, then slice into rounds.

Place one sheet of dough on the bottom of a pie pan. Place a layer of rapini, then sausage slices, and sprinkling of cheese. Repeat until pan is full. Cover with second sheet of dough. Cut a few vents, and brush top with the lightly beaten egg. Bake for 20 to 30 minutes until golden brown.

FETTUCCINE ALL'ARAGOSTA CON FRUTTI DI MARE
{LOBSTER & SEAFOOD FETTUCCINE}

serves 4

- 4 whole Maine lobsters
- 1 finely chopped shallot
- 4 tablespoons good-quality olive oil
- 4 pounds mussels, clams and rock shrimp
- ½ cup brandy
- 2 cups heavy cream

- Optional for richer sauce: ½ teaspoon lobster or shrimp base or bouillon *(see resources page 96)*
- Salt and freshly ground pepper to taste
- 1 pound dried egg noodle fettuccine
- Garnish: Fresh basil

In a large stockpot, steam lobsters for 3 to 5 minutes each. Cut lobsters in half lengthwise; crack claws. In a large sauté or frying pan over medium heat, sauté shallots in olive oil, until golden brown. Add shellfish, cover three quarters, and cook until shellfish open. Discard any that do not open. Add shrimp and lobster, cooking for a couple more minutes. Add brandy and flame. Once alcohol has burned off and flame has subsided, stir in heavy cream and lobster base, if using. Season with salt and freshly ground pepper to taste.

Meanwhile, cook the pasta in a large pot of boiling salted water until al dente. Drain the pasta lightly, leaving it slightly wet. Add the cooked pasta to the sauce and shellfish in the sauté pan, and toss until the sauce coats the pasta.

To plate: Add a serving of pasta to a plate. Top with 1 lobster along with shellfish, shrimp and sauce. Garnish with fresh basil.

index of recipes

RESOURCES

Have a question? Want to make your home cooking even easier? Please call or stop by Cicciotti's Trattoria {1933 South Elijo Ave., Cardiff, CA 92007. (760) 634-2335. www.cicciottis.com} to talk to Gaetano or to purchase any of his freshly made Italian specialties — sauces, pasta, bread or any dish on his menu is also available to go.

- **Fresh pasta:** *Available at Cicciotti's Trattoria, Italian specialty stores, or online at www.freshpasta.com.*
- **Lobster, shrimp and chicken base or bouillon:** *Available at local grocery or specialty food stores.*
- **Seafood, meat and other specialty items:** *Available at Cardiff Seaside Market {www.seasidemarket.com} or Trader Joe's {www.traderjoes.com}.*